# debbie macomber

Debbie Macomber's popular Blossom Street series continues to delight her fans with its carefully crafted stories of love and friendship. With more than 60 million copies of Debbie's books in print, her compelling characters have touched hearts all over the world.

Debbie's marvelous books aren't the only way she shares her talent with others. Debbie is an avid knitter who believes strongly in "giving back" to her community. One way she accomplishes this is by drawing attention to worthy causes through her books.

While working on her popular novel, *The Shop on Blossom Street*, Debbie learned about an organization called *Warm Up America!* This charity group consists of knitters and crocheters who create 7" x 9" blocks which are joined into blankets for the needy. Debbie became one of the first board members for Warm Up America!, and she continues to work tirelessly on its behalf. Debbie urges everyone who uses these patterns to take a few minutes to knit or crochet a block for this cause. See page 40 to find out how you can make a real difference.

Debbie also hopes that **this collection of ten fun and stylish fashions** will inspire you to discover the rich rewards of knitting for yourself and those you love.

LEISURE ARTS, INC.
Little Rock, Arkansas

# a word from LEISURE ARTS and MIRA books

## Read The Books that Inspired the Projects

As many of Debbie Macomber's fans know, the fascinating characters in her stories are often knitters who create thoughtful gifts for their loved ones. To help you experience the rewards of knitting just like your favorite Blossom Street characters, Leisure Arts is excited to offer the latest companion publication to the popular book series. *Knit Along with Debbie Macomber—Back on Blossom Street* is filled with knitting patterns inspired by the story.

You'll discover excerpts from Debbie's books and enjoy creating five prayer shawls, a knitted lace wedding invitation, beanie cap, infant romper, cardigan, and a scarf set. Also included is a pattern for a sample block that you can make to contribute to Debbie's favorite nonprofit organization, *Warm Up America!*

For more knitting fun with Debbie, look for these Leisure Arts instruction books: *Knit Along with Debbie Macomber—The Shop on Blossom Street, Knit Along with Debbie Macomber—A Good Yarn,* and *Knit Along with Debbie Macomber—The Cedar Cove Collection.*

Read all of Debbie's heartwarming stories, then knit up a little creativity from Leisure Arts.

**knit** along with
DEBBIE MACOMBER

LOOK FOR DEBBIE'S HEARTWARMING STORIES AT BOOKSTORES EVERYWHERE, AND COLLECT ALL FOUR KNITTING PUBLICATIONS INSPIRED BY HER BLOSSOM STREET AND CEDAR COVE NOVELS.

Leaflet# 4658

Leaflet# 4132

Leaflet# 4135

To find out more about Debbie Macomber, visit www.debbiemacomber.com or www.mirabooks.com.

For information about these and other Leisure Arts publications call 1.800.526.5111 or visit www.leisurearts.com.

LEISURE ARTS
*the art of everyday living*

2

# meet the women

## from *Back on Blossom Street*

## Lydia Goetz

*I*'m grateful for every minute I spend in my shop on Blossom Street in downtown Seattle. Even now, after ten years of living cancer-free, knitting dominates my life. Because of my yarn store, I've become part of a community of knitters and friends. And I've decided it's time to start another knitting class. I usually begin a new session four or five times a year. Lately, I've seen several patterns for prayer shawls, some more complex than others. Prayer shawls offer comfort and warmth, emotional, as well as physical. I've received several inquiries about them and think perhaps one of these shawls would make for an interesting class.

# Alix Townsend

Alix needed a cigarette. Bad. In less than four months, she would become Reverend Jordan Turner's wife, and frankly, that terrified her. Alix Townsend, a pastor's wife! Her mother was in prison. Her only brother was dead of a drug overdose, and she'd had no contact with her father in twelve years. Alix didn't consider herself a fancy-church-wedding candidate, but somehow, she'd become immersed in this whole crazy sideshow of a wedding. Most of the time Alix's wishes for the wedding were ignored. And she couldn't shake the feeling that she was a disappointment to her future mother-in-law.

"You need something to take your mind off all this wedding business," Jordan said. "What about another knitting class?"

Alix nodded slowly. "Lydia's starting a new class for a prayer shawl. I'll sign up for the class after work." She did her best to remember that a big fancy event would make Jordan's parents happy. Because, more than anything, Alix wanted to be Jordan's wife. She just had to survive the wedding first.

# Colette Blake

There's a new shop on Seattle's Blossom Street—a flower store called *Susannah's Garden*, right next door to A Good Yarn. Susannah Nelson, the owner, has just hired a young widow named Colette Blake, who's currently living in the apartment over the knit shop. A couple of months earlier, Colette had abruptly quit her previous job—after a brief affair with her boss. To her dismay, he's suddenly begun placing weekly orders for flower arrangements! Susannah and Colette have both joined Lydia Goetz's new knitting class. With so much to think about, Colette is surprised to discover herself actually looking forward to her first knitting class. Surely knitting will bring her some much-needed peace and contentment!

# beginner's
# prayer shawl

*Lydia is excited about teaching this simple prayer shawl pattern in her latest beginner's class. The woven appearance of the border is created by knitting three, then purling three. And like many knitting patterns, this one offers versatility. With just a change in color, the prayer shawl would be perfect for a baby blanket.*

■■□□ **EASY**

**Finished Size:** 31" x 43½" (78.5 cm x 110.5 cm)

## MATERIALS
Bulky Weight Yarn **(5 BULKY)**
[3½ ounces, 148 yards
(100 grams, 136 meters) per skein]:
  7 skeins
 31" (78.5 cm) Circular knitting needle,
  size 10 (6 mm) **or** size needed for gauge

**GAUGE:** In Garter Stitch (knit every row),
       14 sts and 26 rows = 4" (10 cm)

## BOTTOM BORDER
Cast on 111 sts.

**Row 1:** K3, (P3, K3) across.

**Row 2:** P3, (K3, P3) across.

**Rows 3 and 4:** Repeat Rows 1 and 2.

**Row 5:** P3, (K3, P3) across.

**Row 6:** K3, (P3, K3) across.

**Rows 7 and 8:** Repeat Rows 5 and 6.

**Rows 9-12:** Repeat Rows 1-4.

## BODY
**Row 1:** P3, K3, P3, knit across to last 9 sts, P3, K3, P3.

**Row 2:** K3, P3, knit across to last 6 sts, P3, K3.

**Row 3:** P3, K3, P3, knit across to last 9 sts, P3, K3, P3.

**Row 4:** K3, P3, K6, YO *(Fig. 1a, page 44)*, K2 tog *(Fig. 5, page 45)*, (K3, YO, K2 tog) across to last 12 sts, K6, P3, K3.

**Row 5:** K3, P3, knit across to last 6 sts, P3, K3.

**Row 6:** P3, K3, P3, knit across to last 9 sts, P3, K3, P3.

**Row 7:** K3, P3, knit across to last 6 sts, P3, K3.

**Row 8:** P3, K3, P3, K5, YO, K2 tog, (K3, YO, K2 tog) across to last 15 sts, K6, P3, K3, P3.

Repeat Rows 1-8 for pattern until piece measures approximately 41" (104 cm) from cast on edge, ending by working Row 3.

**Next Row:** K3, P3, knit across to last 6 sts, P3, K3.

## TOP BORDER
Repeat Rows 1-12 of Bottom Border.

Bind off all sts in pattern.

I pointed out that the border of the Beginner's Prayer Shawl was knit in a seed pattern of knit three, purl three. "I bet the three stitches are significant," Colette murmured as she switched the yarn from the back to the front in order to purl.

"Faith, hope, love," Alix stated in a thoughtful tone. "Mind, body, spirit," Susannah said. "Past, present, future," Colette threw in. I wondered again if living day to day was all she could handle.

—Lydia
*Back on Blossom Street*

# baby's hooded cardigan

*Pure sweetness! Every baby deserves a darling "hoodie" like this one. The pattern is proving to be popular with Lydia's customers. And who wouldn't have fun working with a rainbow of soft yarn colors?*

◼◼◼◻ **INTERMEDIATE**

| Size | Finished Chest Measurement |
|------|---------------------------|
| 6 months | 22" (56 cm) |
| 12 months | 23" (59.5 cm) |
| 18 months | 25" (63.5 cm) |

***Note:*** Instructions are written for size 6 months, with sizes 12 & 18 months in braces { }. Instructions will be easier to read if you circle all the numbers pertaining to your infant's size. If only one number is given, it applies to all sizes.

## MATERIALS

Double Knitting Weight Yarn
[1³/₄ ounces, 186 yards
(50 grams, 170 meters) per skein]:
   White - 3{4-5} skeins
   6 Contrasting Colors - 1 skein **each** color
      (we used Baby Blue, Pale Yellow, Peach,
      Lt Green, Lavender, and Baby Pink)
Straight knitting needles, sizes 4 (3.5 mm)
   **and** 6 (4 mm) **or** sizes needed for gauge
Stitch holders - 2
¹/₂" (12 mm) Buttons - 6{6-8}
Yarn needle

**GAUGE:** With larger size knitting needles,
   in Body pattern,
   23 sts and 32 rows = 4" (10 cm)

---

Cardigan is worked in one piece to underarm.

## BODY
### RIBBING
With White and smaller size knitting needles, cast on 115{121-133} sts **loosely**.

**Row 1:** P2, K1, (P1, K1) across to last 2 sts, P2.

**Row 2** (Right side): K2, P1, (K1, P1) across to last 2 sts, K2.

**Rows 3-10:** Repeat Rows 1 and 2, 4 times.

**Row 11:** Work across increasing 8{10-10} sts evenly spaced across (**see Increases, page 45**): 123{131-143} sts.

## BODY
Change to larger size knitting needles.

**Rows 1-4:** Beginning with a **knit** row, work in Stockinette Stitch (knit one row, purl one row) for 4 rows.

When instructed to slip a stitch, always slip as if to **purl** unless instructed otherwise. Carry yarn **loosely** along the **wrong** side of the work when slipping stitches.

**Row 5:** Slip 3{1-5}, with next new color K5{3-5}, (slip 3, K5) across to last 3{7-5} sts, (slip 3, K3) 0{1-0} time(s) (**see Zeros, page 42**), leave remaining 3{1-5} st(s) unworked; **turn**.

*Instructions continued on page 10.*

Something else I love about knitting—when I'm working with my needles and yarn, I link myself with hundreds of thousands of women through the centuries.

—Lydia
*Back on Blossom Street*

9

**Row 6:** K5{3-5}, (slip 3, K5) across to last 3{7-5} sts, (slip 3, K3) 0{1-0} time(s), slip last 3{1-5} sts; cut new color.

**Rows 7-12:** With White, work in Stockinette Stitch for 6 rows.

**Row 13:** Slip 1{3-1}, with next new color K3{5-5}, slip 3, (K5, slip 3) across to last 4{8-6} sts, K3{5-5}, leave remaining 1{3-1} st(s) unworked; **turn**.

**Row 14:** K3{5-5}, slip 3, (K5, slip 3) across to last 4{8-6} sts, K3{5-5}, slip 1{3-1}; cut new color.

**Rows 15-20:** With White, work in Stockinette Stitch for 6 rows.

Repeat Rows 5-20 for pattern until piece measures approximately 6$\frac{1}{2}${7$\frac{1}{2}$-8$\frac{1}{2}$}"/ 16.5{19-21.5} cm from cast on edge, ending by working Row 6 or Row 14.

## RIGHT FRONT
**Row 1:** With White K 29{31-34}, slip next 65{69-75} sts onto first st holder for Back, slip remaining 29{31-34} sts onto second st holder for Left Front: 29{31-34} sts.

**Rows 2-4:** Work in Stockinette Stitch for 3 rows.

**Row 5:** With next new color K2, (slip 3, K1) across to last 3{5-0} sts, slip 2{3-0}, K1{2-0}.

**Row 6:** P1{3-2}, (slip 1, K3) across.

**Row 7:** Knit across.

**Row 8:** Purl across.

Repeat Rows 5-8 for pattern until piece measures approximately 9$\frac{1}{2}${10$\frac{3}{4}$-12}"/ 24{27.5-30.5} cm from cast on edge, ending by working a **wrong** side row.

## NECK SHAPING
Maintain established pattern throughout.

**Row 1:** Bind off 5{6-6} sts, work across: 24{25-28} sts.

**Row 2:** Work across.

**Row 3** (Decrease row): Slip 1 as if to **knit**, K1, PSSO (*Figs. 7a & b, page 46*), work across: 23{24-27} sts.

Repeat Rows 2 and 3, 2{2-3} times: 21{22-24} sts.

Work even until Right Front measures approximately 11{12$\frac{1}{2}$-14}"/28{32-35.5} cm from cast on edge, ending by working a **wrong** side row.

Bind off all remaining sts.

## BACK
With **right** side facing, slip 65{69-75} sts from Back st holder onto an empty larger size knitting needle.

**Rows 1-4:** With White, work in Stockinette Stitch for 4 rows.

**Row 5:** With next new color K1{1-2}, slip 3, (K1, slip 3) across to last 1{1-2} st(s), K1{1-2}.

**Row 6:** P2{2-3}, slip 1, (P3, slip 1) across to last 2{2-3} sts, P2{2-3}.

**Row 7:** Knit across.

**Row 8:** Purl across.

Repeat Rows 5-8 for pattern until Back measures same as Right Front, ending by working a **wrong** side row.

Bind off first 21{22-24} sts, work across until there are 23{25-27} sts on the right knitting needle, slip these 23{25-27} sts onto the st holder; bind off remaining sts.

## LEFT FRONT

With **right** side facing, slip 29{31-34} sts from Left Front st holder onto an empty larger size knitting needle.

**Rows 1-4:** With White, work in Stockinette Stitch for 4 rows.

**Row 5:** With next new color K1{2-1}, slip 2{3-3}, (K1, slip 3) across to last 2 sts, K2.

**Row 6:** (P3, slip 1) across to last 1{3-2} st(s), P1{3-2}.

**Row 7:** Knit across.

**Row 8:** Purl across.

Repeat Rows 5-8 until Left Front measures same as Right Front to Neck Shaping, ending by working a **right** side row.

### NECK SHAPING
**Row 1:** Bind off 5{6-6} sts, work across: 24{25-28} sts.

**Row 2** (Decrease row)**:** Work across to last 2 sts, K2 tog **(Fig. 5, page 45)**: 23{24-27} sts.

**Row 3:** Work across.

Repeat Rows 2 and 3, 2{2-3} times: 21{22-24} sts.

Work even until Left Front measures same as Right Front, ending by working a **wrong** side row.

Bind off remaining sts.

Sew shoulder seams.

*Instructions continued on page 34.*

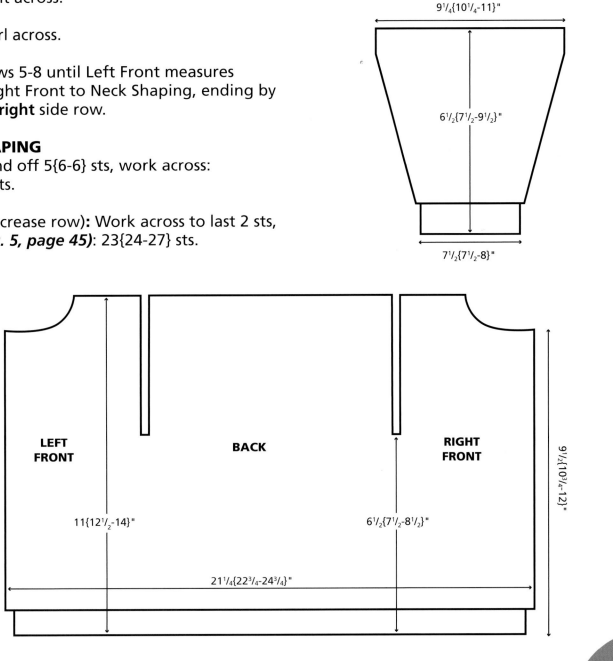

# welcome
## little onesie

*Now, who could be the recipient of this baby gift from Lydia? If you want to find out, you'll have to ask Lydia. In the meantime, perhaps you'd like to knit a romper like this one for a little someone you know? The cable design on the bodice and the soft, dotted yarn makes the whole garment seem like a celebration.*

▰▰▰▰▱ **INTERMEDIATE**

| Size | Finished Chest Measurement |
|---|---|
| 3 months | 18" (45.5 cm) |
| 6 months | 20" (51 cm) |
| 12 months | 21" (53.5 cm) |
| 18 months | 22" (56 cm) |

*Note:* Instructions are written for size 3 months, with sizes 6, 12, & 18 months in braces { }. Instructions will be easier to read if you circle all the numbers pertaining to your infant's size. If only one number is given, it applies to all sizes.

## MATERIALS

Double Knitting Weight Yarn
[1³/₄ ounces, 186 yards
(50 grams, 170 meters) per skein]:
    Spot Print - 3{3-4-4} skeins
    Peach, Mint, Yellow and Blue -
      1{1-2-2} skeins **each** color
16" (40.5 cm) **or** 24" (61 cm) Circular knitting
    needle, size 5 (3.75 mm) **or** size needed
    for gauge
Straight knitting needles, size 3 (3.25 mm)
Cable needle
Stitch holders - 3
Markers
¹/₂" (12 mm) Buttons - 3
Snap tape - 12{14-16-18}"/
    30.5{35.5-40.5-45.5} cm length
Yarn needle
Sewing needle and matching thread

**GAUGE:** With circular knitting needle,
    in Stockinette Stitch,
      24 sts and 32 rows = 4" (10 cm)

## STITCH GUIDE

**CABLE 2 BACK** *(abbreviated C2B)*
Slip next 2 sts onto cable needle and hold in **back** of work, K2 from left needle, K2 from cable needle.

**CABLE 2 FRONT** *(abbreviated C2F)*
Slip next 2 sts onto cable needle and hold in **front** of work, K2 from left needle, K2 from cable needle.

## FIRST LEG
### RIBBING

With Blue and straight knitting needles, cast on 38{40-40-42} sts **loosely**.

Work in K1, P1 ribbing for 1¹/₂" (4 cm) increasing 4{6-4-2} sts evenly spaced across last row *(see Increases, page 45)*: 42{46-44-44} sts.

## BODY

Change to circular knitting needle.

**Row 1** (Right side)**:** With Spot Print, knit across.

**Row 2:** Purl across.

**Rows 3 and 4:** Repeat Rows 1 and 2.

**Row 5:** Increase in first st *(Figs. 3a & b, page 45)*, knit across to last 2 sts, increase in next st, K1: 44{48-46-46} sts.

*Instructions continued on page 14.*

I'd been on an emotional high ever since I heard the news. A new baby pattern book had arrived earlier in the week, and I planned to knit a project out of it. I could envision a reunion of my first knitting class in a few months. We would have hand-knit gifts to welcome this new baby.

—Lydia
*Back on Blossom Street*

13

Working in Stockinette Stitch, continue to increase in same manner, every fourth row, 0{2-4-6} times **more** *(see Zeros, page 42)*; then increase every sixth row, 4 times: 52{60-62-66} sts.

Work even until piece measures approximately 5$\frac{1}{2}${6$\frac{1}{2}$-7$\frac{1}{2}$-8$\frac{1}{2}$}"/14{16.5-19-21.5} cm from cast on edge, ending by working a **purl** row.

### SHAPING
**Row 1 (Increase row):** Increase in first st, knit across: 53{61-63-67} sts.

**Row 2:** Purl across.

**Rows 3 and 4:** Repeat Rows 1 and 2: 54{62-64-68} sts.

**Row 5:** Add on 7{6-7-7} sts **loosely** *(Figs. 2a & b, page 44)*: 61{68-71-75} sts.

Slip sts onto a st holder.

## SECOND LEG
Work same as First Leg to Shaping: 52{60-62-66} sts.

### SHAPING
**Row 1 (Increase row):** Knit across to last 2 sts, increase in next st, K1: 53{61-63-67} sts.

**Row 2:** Purl across.

**Rows 3 and 4:** Repeat Rows 1 and 2: 54{62-64-68} sts.

**Row 5:** Increase in first st, knit across; slip sts from the First Leg st holder onto the opposite end of the circular knitting needle, knit across to last 2 sts, increase in next st, K1: 117{132-137-145} sts.

**Row 6:** Purl across.

**Row 7:** Increase in first st, knit across to last 2 sts, increase in next st, K1: 119{134-139-147} sts.

**Row 8:** Purl across; cut yarn.

## BODY
With **right** side facing, slip first 56{64-66-70} sts to opposite end of circular knitting needle, place a marker to mark the beginning of the round *(see Markers, page 42)*, with Spot Print knit across remaining 63{70-73-77} sts, **turn**; add on 7{6-7-7} sts, **turn**; knit around to marker: 126{140-146-154} sts.

Knit every round until Body measures approximately 7{8$\frac{3}{4}$-10$\frac{1}{2}$-12$\frac{1}{4}$}"/ 18{22-26.5-31} cm from last added on sts.

**Next Rnd:** K3{3-4-3}, K2 tog *(Fig. 5, page 45)*, ★ K5{5-6-5}, K2 tog; repeat from ★ around to last 2{2-4-2} sts, K2{2-4-2}: 108{120-128-132} sts.

**Next Rnd:** Purl around.

**Next Rnd:** Knit around.

**Next Rnd (Garter ridge):** Purl around.

## LEFT BACK YOKE
**Row 1:** Bind off 6 sts, K9, with Peach K8, with Spot Print K6{9-11-12}, slip next 54{60-64-66} sts onto first st holder for Front, slip remaining 24{27-29-30} sts onto second st holder for Right Back Yoke: 24{27-29-30} sts.

**Row 2:** P5{8-10-11}, K1, with Peach P8, with Spot Print K1, purl across.

**Row 3:** K 10, with Peach C2B, C2F, with Spot Print knit across.

**Row 4:** P5{8-10-11}, K1, with Peach P8, with Spot Print K1, purl across.

**Row 5:** K 10, with Peach K8, with Spot knit across.

**Rows 6-8:** Repeat Rows 4 and 5 once, then repeat Row 4 once **more**.

Repeat Rows 3-8 until Left Back Yoke measures approximately 3$\frac{1}{4}${3$\frac{1}{2}$-3$\frac{3}{4}$-4}"/8.5{9-9.5-10} cm from Garter ridge, ending by working a **wrong** side row.

## NECK SHAPING
**Row 1:** K5{7-7-7}, slip sts just worked onto a st holder, work across: 19{20-22-23} sts.

**Row 2:** Work across.

**Row 3:** SSK *(Figs. 6a-c, page 45)*, work across: 18{19-21-22} sts.

**Row 4:** Work across.

Bind off remaining sts in pattern.

## FRONT YOKE
With **right** side facing, slip 54{60-64-66} sts from Front st holder onto circular knitting needle.

**Row 1:** With Spot Print K6{9-11-12}, with Peach K8, with Spot Print K9, with Mint K8, with Spot Print K9, with Yellow K8, with Spot Print knit across.

**Row 2:** P5{8-10-11}, K1, with Yellow P8, with Spot Print K1, P7, K1, with Mint P8, with Spot Print, K1, P7, K1, with Peach P8, with Spot Print K1, purl across.

**Row 3:** K6{9-11-12}, with Peach C2B, C2F, with Spot Print K9, with Mint C2B, C2F, with Spot Print K9, with Yellow C2B, C2F, with Spot Print knit across.

**Row 4:** P5{8-10-11}, K1, with Yellow P8, with Spot Print K1, P7, K1, with Mint P8, with Spot Print, K1, P7, K1, with Peach P8, with Spot Print K1, purl across.

**Rows 5-8:** Repeat Rows 1 and 2 twice.

Repeat Rows 3-8 until Front Yoke measures approximately 2{2-2$\frac{1}{4}$-2$\frac{1}{4}$}"/5{5-5.5-5.5} cm from Garter ridge, ending by working a **wrong** side row.

## NECK SHAPING
Both sides of Neck are worked at the same time, using separate yarns for **each** side.

**Row 1** (Right side)**:** Work across 21{22-24-25} sts, slip next 12{16-16-16} sts onto a st holder; with separate yarns, work across: 21{22-24-25} sts **each** side.

**Row 2:** Work across; with separate yarns, work across.

**Row 3** (Decrease row)**:** Work across to within 2 sts of Neck edge, K2 tog; with separate yarns, SSK, work across: 20{21-23-24} sts **each** side.

**Rows 4-7:** Repeat Rows 2 and 3 twice: 18{19-21-22} sts **each** side.

Work even until Front Yoke measures same as Left Back Yoke, ending by working a **wrong** side row.

Bind off remaining sts in pattern.

## RIGHT BACK YOKE
With **right** side facing, slip sts from Right Back Yoke st holder onto circular knitting needle: 24{27-29-30} sts.

**Row 1** (Right side)**:** With Spot Print K6{9-11-12}, with Yellow K8, with Spot Print knit across.

**Row 2:** P9, K1, with Yellow P8, with Spot Print K1, purl across.

**Row 3:** K6{9-11-12}, with Yellow C2B, C2F, with Spot Print knit across.

**Row 4:** P9, K1, with Yellow P8, with Spot Print K1, purl across.

**Rows 5-8:** Repeat Rows 1 and 2 twice.

Repeat Rows 3-8 until Right Back Yoke measures 3$\frac{1}{4}${3$\frac{1}{2}$-3$\frac{3}{4}$-4}"/8.5{9-9.5-10} cm from Garter ridge, ending by working a **right** side row.

*Instructions continued on page 38.*

# knitted beanie

*Fast to finish—that's a nice thing to be able to say about any knitting project. Lydia has two men in her life—her husband and her stepson—who can benefit from these quick-knit caps. Knowing Lydia, they probably have several of these caps in colors to go with everything. Not that Brad and Cody are all that concerned with coordinating their outfits, mind you!*

●■■□□ **EASY**

**Finished Size:** One size fits most adults

## MATERIALS

Medium Weight Yarn
[3.52 ounces, 166 yards
(100 grams, 152 meters) per skein]:
   2 skeins
Straight knitting needles, size 8 (5 mm) **or**
   size needed for gauge
Yarn needle

**GAUGE:** In Stockinette Stitch,
   19 sts and 26 rows = 4" (10 cm)
   In pattern,
   23 sts and 26 rows = 4" (10 cm)

## BEANIE
### ROLLED BRIM
Cast on 115 sts **loosely**.

Beginning with a **knit** row, work in Stockinette Stitch (knit one row, purl one row) until piece measures approximately 1¹/₂" (4 cm) from cast on edge, ending by working a **purl** row.

## BODY
**Row 1** (Right side): P2, K1, (P5, K1) across to last 4 sts, P4.

**Row 2:** K4, P1, (K5, P1) across to last 2 sts, K2.

Repeat Rows 1 and 2 until Body measures approximately 6" (15 cm), ending by working Row 2.

### SHAPING
**Row 1:** P1, K2 tog *(Fig. 5, page 45)*, ★ P2 tog twice *(Fig. 10, page 46)*, K2 tog; repeat from ★ across to last 4 sts, P2 tog, P2: 59 sts.

**Row 2:** K3, P1, (K2, P1) across to last st, K1.

**Row 3:** P1, K1, (P2, K1) across to last 3 sts, P3.

**Row 4:** K3, P1, (K2, P1) across to last st, K1.

**Row 5:** P1, (K1, P2 tog) across to last st, P1: 40 sts.

Cut yarn, leaving a long end for sewing.

Thread the yarn needle with the long end and run the needle through the remaining sts twice, pulling the yarn tightly; secure the end but do **not** cut the yarn. With the needle and the remaining yarn, sew the hat seam, reversing the seam at the Rolled Brim; tack the bottom of the Rolled Brim at Row 1 of Body.

I know machines can create sweaters and mittens and other things cheaper, faster and far more efficiently. That's not the point. The projects I knit are an extension of me, an expression of my love for the person I'm knitting for.

—Lydia
*Back on Blossom Street*

# you're invited

*These wedding invitations are simply romantic, and Alix wouldn't have them any other way. She knitted the lace herself, and Jordan even helped her to create the cards. But will Alix's friend Jacqueline—and Jordan's mother Susan—agree to let the young couple use their creations?*

■□□□□ EXPERIENCED

**Finished Size:** 2¼"w x 7¾"h
(5.5 cm x 19.5 cm)

## MATERIALS
Bedspread Weight Cotton Thread, size 10:
25 yards (23 meters)
Straight knitting needles, size 1 (2.25 mm)
Wedding invitation
Tapestry needle

## EDGING
Cast on 15 sts.

**Row 1:** K2, purl across to last 2 sts, K2.

See Yarn Overs, page 44, and Decreases, pages 45 & 46.

**Row 2** (Right side)**:** K2, (YO, SSK) 3 times, K1, (K2 tog, YO) twice, K2.

**Row 3:** K2, purl across to last 2 sts, K2.

**Row 4:** K2, YO, K1, (YO, SSK) 3 times, (K2 tog, YO) twice, K2: 16 sts.

**Row 5:** K2, purl across to last 2 sts, K2.

**Row 6:** K2, YO, K3, (YO, SSK) twice, K1, (K2 tog, YO) twice, K2: 17 sts.

**Row 7:** K2, purl across to last 2 sts, K2.

**Row 8:** K2, YO, K5, (YO, SSK) twice, (K2 tog, YO) twice, K2: 18 sts.

**Row 9:** K2, purl across to last 2 sts, K2.

**Row 10:** K2, YO, K7, YO, SSK, K1, (K2 tog, YO) twice, K2: 19 sts.

**Row 11:** K2, purl across to last 2 sts, K2.

**Row 12:** K2, YO, K9, YO, SSK, (K2 tog, YO) twice, K2: 20 sts.

**Row 13:** K2, purl across to last 2 sts, K2.

**Row 14:** K1, SSK, YO, SSK, K2 tog, YO, K1, YO, SSK, K2 tog, YO, SSK, (K2 tog, YO) twice, K2: 18 sts.

**Row 15:** K2, P6, P2 tog, P3, P2 tog tbl, P1, K2: 16 sts.

**Row 16:** K1, SSK, (YO, SSK) 3 times, K1, (K2 tog, YO) twice, K2: 15 sts.

**Row 17:** K2, purl across to last 2 sts, K2.

**Rows 18-87:** Repeat Rows 4-17, 5 times.

Bind off all sts in **knit**.

## FINISHING
Weave in thread ends.
Block the piece the length of the Invitation if needed. Attach piece to edge of Invitation.

"Alix and I spent the weekend creating our own wedding invitations," said Jordan. "Each is handmade."

"You made these?" Jacqueline took a card. "They're exceptional. I love the way you've incorporated the hand-knitted lace."

—from *Back on Blossom Street*

With joyous hearts,
Alix Townsend
and
Jordan Turner
request the pleasure of
your company as they
exchange marriage vows.
Saturday, June 2, 2007
2 o'clock in the afternoon
The Turner Cabin
Star Lake, Washington
Reception to follow

# seattle chill chasers

*Winter in Seattle is as wet as it is chilly, so it makes sense to be prepared with a set of cold-weather accessories. Besides, it's fun to knit up this set of mock-cabled mittens with their matching scarf and hat. Jacqueline, one of Lydia's first customers, has plans to make this set for her daugher-in-law, Tammie Lee. And since Alix is like a daughter to Jacqueline, she may also end up with her own cozy set.*

◼◼◼◻ INTERMEDIATE

## MATERIALS
Medium Weight Yarn
[3.5 ounces, 195 yards
(100 grams, 175 meters) per skein]:
  **Entire Set** - 5 skeins
  **Scarf** - 3 skeins
  **Hat** - 1 skein
  **Mittens** - 1 skein
Straight knitting needles, sizes 5 (3.75 mm)
  **and** 7 (4.5 mm) **or** sizes needed for gauge
Yarn needle
Crochet hook (to fringe Scarf)

**GAUGE:** With larger size needles, in pattern,
29 sts and 26 rows = 4" (10 cm)

## SCARF
**Finished Size:** 6¹/₂" x 67" (16.5 cm x 170 cm)

With larger size knitting needles, cast on 47 sts.

**Row 1:** K2, (P3, K2) across.

**Row 2** (Right side)**:** P2, (K3, P2) across.

**Row 3:** K2, (P3, K2) across.

**Row 4:** P2, ★ [slip 1 as if to **knit**, K2, PSSO *(Fig. 9, page 46)*], P2; repeat from ★ across: 38 sts.

**Row 5:** K2, ★ P1, YO *(Fig. 1b, page 44)*, P1, K2; repeat from ★ across: 47 sts.

Repeat Rows 2-5 for pattern until Scarf measures approximately 67" (170 cm) from cast on edge, ending by working Row 3.

Bind off all sts in pattern.

Holding 4 strands of yarn together, each 11" (28 cm) long, add fringe to center of each "cable" across both short ends of Scarf *(Figs. 15a & b, page 47)*.

## HAT
**Finished Size:** One size fits most adults

With larger size knitting needles,
cast on 97 sts **loosely**.

**Row 1:** K2, (P3, K2) across.

**Row 2** (Right side): P2, (K3, P2) across.

**Row 3:** K2, (P3, K2) across.

**Row 4:** P2, ★ [slip 1 as if to **knit**, K2, PSSO *(Fig. 9, page 46)*], P2; repeat from ★ across: 78 sts.

**Row 5:** K2, ★ P1, YO *(Fig. 1b, page 44)*, P1, K2; repeat from ★ across: 97 sts.

**Rows 6-53:** Repeat Rows 2-5, 12 times: 97 sts.

*Instructions continued on page 33.*

Knitting had proven to be a turning point in Alix's life. "After a while, I got the hang of it. I found that if I had something on my mind, it helped to sit down and knit. If I could free my mind for even a few minutes, I could sometimes settle whatever was bothering me."

—from *Back on Blossom Street*

21

# lap robe

*Lydia is truly worried about her sister. The normally outspoken Margaret has become withdrawn and angry ever since her daughter experienced a traumatic event. It's Lydia's hope that Margaret will be able to work past some of her anger while knitting this prayer shawl that can also serve as a lap robe.*

■■■□ INTERMEDIATE

**Finished Size:** 36" x 50" (91.5 cm x 127 cm)

## MATERIALS

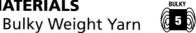

Bulky Weight Yarn
[5 ounces, 255 yards
(140 grams, 233 meters) per skein]:
  6 skeins
31" (78.5 cm) Circular knitting needle,
  size 15 (10 mm) **or** size needed for gauge

Lap Robe is made holding two strands of yarn together.

**GAUGE:** In pattern,
    one repeat (13 sts) = 5" (12.75 cm)
    12 rows = 4$\frac{1}{2}$" (11.5 cm)

## LAP ROBE

Cast on 95 sts.

**Rows 1 and 2:** Knit across.

**Row 3** (Right side)**:** K2, increase *(Figs. 3a & b, page 45)*, K4, [slip 1 as if to **knit**, K2 tog, PSSO *(Fig. 8, page 46)*], K4, ★ increase twice, K4, slip 1 as if to **knit**, K2 tog, PSSO, K4; repeat from ★ across to last 3 sts, increase, K2.

**Row 4:** K2, purl across to last 2 sts, K2.

**Row 5:** K2, increase, K4, slip 1 as if to **knit**, K2 tog, PSSO, K4, ★ increase twice, K4, slip 1 as if to **knit**, K2 tog, PSSO, K4; repeat from ★ across to last 3 sts, increase, K2.

**Row 6:** Knit across.

**Row 7:** K2, increase, K4, slip 1 as if to **knit**, K2 tog, PSSO, K4, ★ increase twice, K4, slip 1 as if to **knit**, K2 tog, PSSO, K4; repeat from ★ across to last 3 sts, increase, K2.

Repeat Rows 4-7 for pattern until Lap Robe measures approximately 49" (124.5 cm) from cast on edge, ending by working Row 5.

**Last 2 Rows:** Knit across.

Bind off all sts in **knit**.

*Designed by Evelyn A. Clark.*

"Why knit a shawl," Margaret asked. "I mean, we could be knitting anything for someone who needs a bit of TLC."

"True." I agreed with her there. "A lap robe or any of a dozen other projects would do just as well."

"Wrapping a shawl around someone is a symbolic embrace." Colette said.

—Lydia
*Back on Blossom Street*

# long on warmth
# prayer shawl

*It wouldn't be surprising if Susannah, the owner of the flower shop next door to A Good Yarn, chose this color to create a prayer shawl for her mother. The one thing Susannah and her ailing mother share in common is a love of flowers, and the spicy hue of this rectangular shawl brings to mind Asian lilies and autumn chrysanthemums. Although probably not a pattern for a beginning knitter, anyone with a little knitting experience will enjoy making this shawl.*

◼◼☐☐ **EASY**

**Finished Size:** 18" x 72" (45.5 cm x 183 cm)

**MATERIALS**

Bulky Weight Yarn
[5 ounces, 153 yards
(140 grams, 140 meters) per skein]:
   5 skeins
Straight knitting needles, size 10¹⁄₂ (6.5 mm)
   **or** size needed for gauge

**GAUGE:** In Stockinette Stitch,
   14 sts and 18 rows = 4" (10 cm)

## SHAWL
Cast on 63 sts.

**Rows 1-10:** Knit across.

**Row 11:** Purl across.

**Row 12 (Right side):** Knit across.

**Rows 13-15:** Repeat Rows 11 and 12 once, then repeat Row 11 once **more**.

**Rows 16-21:** K1, (P1, K1) across.

**Row 22:** Knit across.

**Row 23:** Purl across.

**Rows 24-27:** Repeat Rows 22 and 23 twice.

Repeat Rows 16-27 for pattern until Shawl measures approximately 70" (178 cm) from cast on edge, ending by working Row 25.

**Last 10 Rows:** Knit across.

Bind off all sts in **knit**.

I realized that the act of knitting had already worked its magic on all of us. Alix had come in stressed and ill-tempered, on edge about the wedding. Colette, too, had been nervous and unhappy, for reasons I didn't know. Susannah had her own struggles, launching a new business. We were relaxed now, talking together, laughing, knitting.

—Lydia
*Back on Blossom Street*

25

# three-corner prayer shawl

*Rumor has it, a past member of Lydia's knitting classes is hurrying to make this shawl as a wedding gift for Alix. In the three years since Lydia opened A Good Yarn, Alix's forthright nature has won her true friendships with everyone she's met on Blossom Street.*

■■■▢ **INTERMEDIATE**

**Finished Size:** 58" wide x 40" deep
(147.5 cm x 101.5 cm)

## MATERIALS

Medium Weight Yarn
[3 ounces, 150 yards
(85 grams, 137 meters) per skein]:
6 skeins
31" (78.5 cm) Circular knitting needle,
size 9 (5.5 mm) **or** size needed for gauge

**GAUGE:** In pattern,
18 sts (3 patterns) = 4$\frac{1}{2}$" (11.5 cm)

## SHAWL

Cast on 9 sts **loosely**.

**Rows 1 and 2:** Knit across.

**Row 3** (Right side)**:** P2, YO twice **(see Yarn Overs, page 44)**, separately slip 2 sts as if to **knit (Fig. 6a, page 45)**, P3 tog **(Fig. 12, page 46)**, P2SSO, YO twice, P2: 9 sts.

**Row 4:** K3, P1, K1, P1, K3.

**Rows 5-7:** K2, YO, knit across to last 2 sts, YO, K2: 15 sts.

**Row 8:** Knit across.

**Row 9:** P2, YO twice, separately slip 2 sts as if to **knit**, P3 tog, P2SSO, YO twice, ★ P1, YO twice, separately slip 2 sts as if to **knit**, P3 tog, P2SSO, YO twice; repeat from ★ across to last 2 sts, P2: 15 sts.

**Row 10:** K3, (P1, K1, P1, K3) across.

**Rows 11-13** (Increase rows)**:** K2, YO, knit across to last 2 sts, YO, K2: 21 sts.

Repeat Rows 8-13 for pattern until Shawl measures approximately 40" (101.5 cm) from cast on edge **or to desired length**, ending by working Row 13.

Bind off all sts **loosely** in **knit**.

*Designed by Jeannine LaRoche.*

26

"We should hold a wedding shower for Alix," I said in a rush, wondering why I hadn't thought of it earlier.

"Great idea," Colette said. "Just us—her knitting friends."

Everyone agreed enthusiastically. We discussed knitting-related gifts—pattern books, yarn in a color we knew she liked, a gift certificate for the shop.

—Lydia
*Back on Blossom Street*

# alix's lace prayer shawl

*When Alix decided to sign up for the Prayer Shawl class, Lydia knew her friend would need a more challenging pattern than the one she would teach to everyone else. After all, Alix had been knitting for three years now. This lace shawl offers more variety in its design. And goodness knows, Alix could use the distraction to keep her mind off her upcoming wedding!*

●■■■▷ EXPERIENCED

**Finished Size:** 74" wide x 45" deep
(188 cm x 114.5 cm)

**MATERIALS**
Light Weight Yarn
[4.5 ounces, 360 yards
(130 grams, 329 meters) per skein]:
  3 skeins
31" (78.5 cm) Circular knitting needle,
  size 7 (4.5 mm) **or** size needed for gauge
Straight knitting needle 4 or 5 sizes larger
  than the circular needle (to work bind off)
Yarn/tapestry needle
Markers

**GAUGE:** In pattern,
18 sts (one repeat) = 3³/₄" (9.5 cm)
and 18 rows (one repeat) = 4" (10 cm)

## SHAWL
Cast on 11 sts, leaving a 12" (30.5 cm) length for sewing.

**Setup Row:** K2, P1, K1, P3, K1, P1, K2.

Slip 1 at the beginning of each row as follows: With the yarn in **front** of your working needle, slip the first stitch as if to **purl**, move the yarn to the **back** of the work by passing it between the tips of your needles.

**Row 1** (Right side): Slip 1, K1, P1, K1, YO **(Fig. 1a, page 44)**, K1, YO, place marker **(see Markers, page 42)**, (K1, YO) twice, place marker, K1, P1, K2: 15 sts.

**Row 2 AND ALL WRONG SIDE ROWS:** Slip 1, K1, P1, K1, purl across to last 4 sts, K1, P1, K2.

**Row 3:** Slip 1, K1, P1, K1, YO, K3, YO, K1, YO, K3, YO, K1, P1, K2: 19 sts.

**Row 5:** Slip 1, K1, P1, K1, YO, K5, YO, K1, YO, K5, YO, K1, P1, K2: 23 sts.

**Row 7:** Slip 1, K1, P1, K1, YO, K7, YO, K1, YO, K7, YO, K1, P1, K2: 27 sts.

**Row 9:** Slip 1, K1, P1, K1, YO, K9, YO, K1, YO, K9, YO, K1, P1, K2: 31 sts.

**Row 11:** Slip 1, K1, P1, K1, YO, K 11, YO, K1, YO, K 11, YO, K1, P1, K2: 35 sts.

**Row 13:** Slip 1, K1, P1, K1, YO, K 13, YO, K1, YO, K 13, YO, K1, P1, K2: 39 sts.

**Row 15:** Slip 1, K1, P1, K1, YO, K 15, YO, K1, YO, K 15, YO, K1, P1, K2: 43 sts.

**Row 17:** Slip 1, K1, P1, K1, ★ YO, K1, [YO, slip 1 as if to **knit**, K1, PSSO **(Figs. 7a & b, page 46)**] 3 times, K3, [K2 tog **(Fig. 5, page 45)**, YO] 3 times, K1, YO, K1; repeat from ★ once **more**, P1, K2: 47 sts.

*Instructions continued on page 30.*

This new class, the one to knit a prayer shawl, has a good feel, although I wish more than three people had enrolled. The first person to sign up was Alix Townsend, which surprised me until she mentioned that she needs something to help with the pre-wedding stress.

—Lydia
*Back on Blossom Street*

**Row 19:** Slip 1, K1, P1, K1, ★ YO, K1, (YO, slip 1 as if to **knit**, K1, PSSO) 4 times, K1, (K2 tog, YO) 4 times, K1, YO, K1; repeat from ★ once **more**, P1, K2: 51 sts.

**Row 21:** Slip 1, K1, P1, K1, ★ YO, K3, (YO, slip 1 as if to **knit**, K1, PSSO) 3 times, YO, [slip 1 as if to **knit**, K2 tog, PSSO *(Fig. 8, page 46)*], YO, (K2 tog, YO) 3 times, K3, YO, K1; repeat from ★ once **more**, P1, K2: 55 sts.

**Row 23:** Slip 1, K1, P1, K1, ★ YO, K5, (YO, slip 1 as if to **knit**, K1, PSSO) 3 times, K1, (K2 tog, YO) 3 times, K5, YO, K1; repeat from ★ once **more**, P1, K2: 59 sts.

**Row 25:** Slip 1, K1, P1, K1, ★ YO, K7, (YO, slip 1 as if to **knit**, K1, PSSO) twice, YO, slip 1 as if to **knit**, K2 tog, PSSO, YO, (K2 tog, YO) twice, K7, YO, K1; repeat from ★ once **more**, P1, K2: 63 sts.

**Row 27:** Slip 1, K1, P1, K1, ★ YO, K9, (YO, slip 1 as if to **knit**, K1, PSSO) twice, K1, (K2 tog, YO) twice, K9, YO, K1; repeat from ★ once **more**, P1, K2: 67 sts.

**Row 29:** Slip 1, K1, P1, K1, ★ YO, K 11, YO, slip 1 as if to **knit**, K1, PSSO, YO, slip 1 as if to **knit**, K2 tog, PSSO, YO, K2 tog, YO, K 11, YO, K1; repeat from ★ once **more**, P1, K2: 71 sts.

**Row 31:** Slip 1, K1, P1, K1, ★ YO, K 13, YO, slip 1 as if to **knit**, K1, PSSO, K1, K2 tog, YO, K 13, YO, K1; repeat from ★ once **more**, P1, K2: 75 sts.

**Row 33:** Slip 1, K1, P1, K1, ★ YO, K 15, YO, slip 1 as if to **knit**, K2 tog, PSSO, YO, K 15, YO, K1; repeat from ★ once **more**, P1, K2: 79 sts.

**Row 35:** Slip 1, K1, P1, K1, ★ YO, K1, † (YO, slip 1 as if to **knit**, K1, PSSO) 3 times, K3, (K2 tog, YO) 3 times †, K3, repeat from † to † once, K1, YO, K1; repeat from ★ once **more**, P1, K2: 83 sts.

**Row 37:** Slip 1, K1, P1, K1, ★ YO, K1, † (YO, slip 1 as if to **knit**, K1, PSSO) 4 times, K1, (K2 tog, YO) 4 times, K1 †, repeat from † to † once **more**, YO, K1; repeat from ★ once **more**, P1, K2: 87 sts.

**Row 39:** Slip 1, K1, P1, K1, ★ YO, K3, † (YO, slip 1 as if to **knit**, K1, PSSO) 3 times, YO, slip 1 as if to **knit**, K2 tog, PSSO, YO, (K2 tog, YO) 3 times, K3 †, repeat from † to † once **more**, YO, K1; repeat from ★ once **more**, P1, K2: 91 sts.

**Row 41:** Slip 1, K1, P1, K1, ★ YO, K5, † (YO, slip 1 as if to **knit**, K1, PSSO) 3 times, K1, (K2 tog, YO) 3 times, K5 †, repeat from † to † once **more**, YO, K1; repeat from ★ once **more**, P1, K2: 95 sts.

**Row 43:** Slip 1, K1, P1, K1, ★ YO, K7, † (YO, slip 1 as if to **knit**, K1, PSSO) twice, YO, slip 1 as if to **knit**, K2 tog, PSSO, YO, (K2 tog, YO) twice, K7 †, repeat from † to † once **more**, YO, K1; repeat from ★ once **more**, P1, K2: 99 sts.

**Row 45:** Slip 1, K1, P1, K1, ★ YO, K9, † (YO, slip 1 as if to **knit**, K1, PSSO) twice, K1, (K2 tog, YO) twice, K9 †, repeat from † to † once **more**, YO, K1; repeat from ★ once **more**, P1, K2: 103 sts.

**Row 47:** Slip 1, K1, P1, K1, ★ YO, K 11, † YO, slip 1 as if to **knit**, K1, PSSO, YO, slip 1 as if to **knit**, K2 tog, PSSO, YO, K2 tog, YO, K 11 †, repeat from † to † once **more**, YO, K1; repeat from ★ once **more**, P1, K2: 107 sts.

**Row 49:** Slip 1, K1, P1, K1, ★ YO, K 13, † YO, slip 1 as if to **knit**, K1, PSSO, K1, K2 tog, YO, K 13 †, repeat from † to † once **more**, YO, K1; repeat from ★ once **more**, P1, K2: 111 sts.

**Row 51:** Slip 1, K1, P1, K1, ★ YO, K 15, † YO, slip 1 as if to **knit**, K2 tog, PSSO, YO, K 15 †, repeat from † to † once **more**, YO, K1; repeat from ★ once **more**, P1, K2: 115 sts.

**Row 53:** Slip 1, K1, P1, ★ K1, YO, K1, (YO, slip 1 as if to **knit**, K1, PSSO) 3 times, K3, (K2 tog, YO) 3 times, † K3, (YO, slip 1 as if to **knit**, K1, PSSO) 3 times, K3, (K2 tog, YO) 3 times †, repeat from † to † across to within one st of next marker, K1, YO, slip marker; repeat from ★ once **more**, K1, P1, K2: 119 sts.

**Row 55:** Slip 1, K1, P1, ★ K1, YO, K1, † (YO, slip 1 as if to **knit**, K1, PSSO) 4 times, K1, (K2 tog, YO) 4 times, K1 †, repeat from † to † across to next marker, YO, slip marker; repeat from ★ once **more**, K1, P1, K2: 123 sts.

**Row 57:** Slip 1, K1, P1, ★ K1, YO, K3, † (YO, slip 1 as if to **knit**, K1, PSSO) 3 times, YO, slip 1 as if to **knit**, K2 tog, PSSO, YO, (K2 tog, YO) 3 times, K3 †, repeat from † to † across to next marker, YO, slip marker; repeat from ★ once **more**, K1, P1, K2: 127 sts.

**Row 59:** Slip 1, K1, P1, ★ K1, YO, K5, † (YO, slip 1 as if to **knit**, K1, PSSO) 3 times, K1, (K2 tog, YO) 3 times, K5 †, repeat from † to † across to next marker, YO, slip marker; repeat from ★ once **more**, K1, P1, K2: 131 sts.

**Row 61:** Slip 1, K1, P1, ★ K1, YO, K7, † (YO, slip 1 as if to **knit**, K1, PSSO) twice, YO, slip 1 as if to **knit**, K2 tog, PSSO, YO, (K2 tog, YO) twice, K7 †, repeat from † to † across to next marker, YO, slip marker; repeat from ★ once **more**, K1, P1, K2: 135 sts.

**Row 63:** Slip 1, K1, P1, ★ K1, YO, K9, † (YO, slip 1 as if to **knit**, K1, PSSO) twice, K1, (K2 tog, YO) twice, K9 †, repeat from † to † across to next marker, YO, slip marker; repeat from ★ once **more**, K1, P1, K2: 139 sts.

**Row 65:** Slip 1, K1, P1, ★ K1, YO, K 11, † YO, slip 1 as if to **knit**, K1, PSSO, YO, slip 1 as if to **knit**, K2 tog, PSSO, YO, K2 tog, YO, K 11 †, repeat from † to † across to next marker, YO, slip marker; repeat from ★ once **more**, K1, P1, K2: 143 sts.

**Row 67:** Slip 1, K1, P1, ★ K1, YO, K 13, † YO, slip 1 as if to **knit**, K1, PSSO, K1, K2 tog, YO, K 13 †, repeat from † to † across to next marker, YO, slip marker; repeat from ★ once **more**, K1, P1, K2: 147 sts.

**Row 69:** Slip 1, K1, P1, ★ K1, YO, K 15, † YO, slip 1 as if to **knit**, K2 tog, PSSO, YO, K 15 †, repeat from † to † across to next marker, YO, slip marker; repeat from ★ once **more**, K1, P1, K2: 151 sts.

**Rows 71-214:** Repeat Rows 53-70, 8 times: 439 sts.

## BOTTOM BORDER

**Row 1** (Eyelet row)**:** Slip 1, K1, P1, K1, (YO, K2 tog) across to within one st of next marker, (YO, K1) 3 times, (YO, K2 tog) across to next marker, YO, K1, P1, K2: 443 sts.

**Row 2:** Slip 1, K1, P1, K1, purl across to last 4 sts, K1, P1, K2.

**Row 3:** Slip 1, (K1, P1) across to next marker, cast on one st *(Fig. A)*, slip marker, K1, cast on one st, P1, (K1, P1) across to last 2 sts, K2: 445 sts.

**Fig. A**

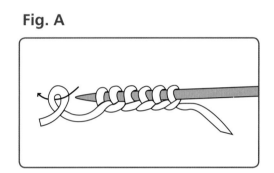

**Row 4:** Slip 1, (K1, P1) across to last 2 sts, K2.

**Row 5:** Slip 1, K1, (P1, K1) across to next marker, cast on one st, slip marker, K1, cast on one st, (K1, P1) across to last 2 sts, K2: 447 sts.

**Row 6:** Slip 1, (K1, P1) across to last 2 sts, K2.

**Row 7:** Slip 1, (K1, P1) across to next marker, cast on one st, slip marker, K1, cast on one st, P1, (K1, P1) across to last 2 sts, K2: 449 sts.

Using a needle 4 or 5 sizes larger for the right needle, bind off all sts **loosely** in pattern.

Thread needle with long end and fold Setup Row in half; sew cast on edge together.

*Designed by Myrna A.I. Stahman.*

# LACY PRAYER SHAWL CHART

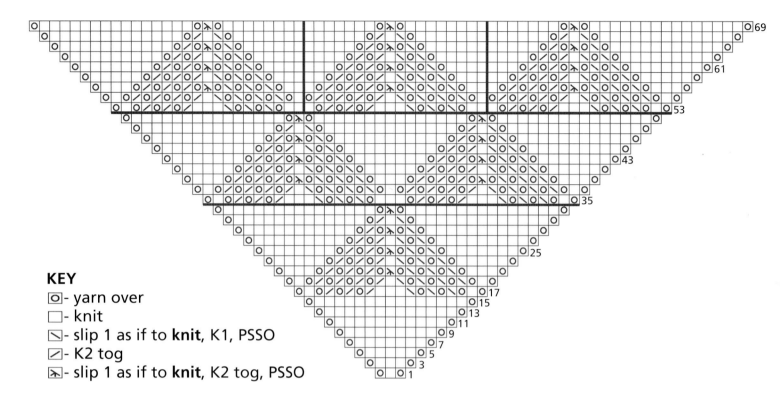

**KEY**

⊡ - yarn over
☐ - knit
◥ - slip 1 as if to **knit**, K1, PSSO
◸ - K2 tog
✱ - slip 1 as if to **knit**, K2 tog, PSSO

The chart is a picture of your knitting as one looks at the public/right side of the shawl. The chart is read from right to left, and from the bottom to the top, just as your knitting progresses. The chart shows only the odd-numbered rows on which the pattern stitches are worked; the even-numbered rows are worked by knitting the knit stitches and purling the purl stitches as they face you.

The chart shows one half of the shawl; it does not show the center stitch that is between and connects the two halves, nor does it show the four border stitches at the beginning and at the end of each row. Work the beginning four border stitches; work the chart one time; knit the one center stitch; work the chart for a second time; work the ending four border stitches.

Repeat Rows 53 through 70, 8 times.
Pattern repeat is between dark vertical lines.

**Row 54:** P2 tog *(Fig. 10, page 46)*, ★ slip 1 as if to **knit**, K2, PSSO, P2 tog; repeat from ★ across: 58 sts.

**Row 55:** K1, (P1, YO, P1, K1) across: 77 sts.

**Row 56:** P1, (K3, P1) across.

**Row 57:** K1, (P3, K1) across.

**Row 58:** P1, ★ [slip 1 as if to **knit**, K2 tog, PSSO *(Fig. 8, page 46)*], P1; repeat from ★ across: 39 sts.

**Row 59:** K1, P2 tog across: 20 sts.

Cut yarn, leaving a long end for sewing. Thread yarn needle with long end and weave through remaining sts to form a ring; pull tightly and secure end, then sew seam from top of Hat to last 4 "cables." Sew remaining seam in reverse. Turn up last 4 "cables" to form cuff.

## MITTEN (Make 2)
**Finished Size:** One size fits most adults

## RIBBING
With smaller size knitting needles, cast on 34 sts **loosely**.

**Row 1:** K2, (P2, K2) across.

**Row 2** (Right side): P2, (K2, P2) across.

Repeat Rows 1 and 2 until Ribbing measures approximately 2¹/₂" (6.5 cm) from cast on edge, ending by working Row 2.

## BODY
**Row 1:** K2, ★ P1, YO *(Fig. 1b, page 44)*, P1, K2; repeat from ★ across: 42 sts.

**Row 2** (Right side): P2, (K3, P2) across.

**Row 3:** K2, (P3, K2) across.

**Row 4:** P2, ★ [slip 1 as if to **knit**, K2, PSSO *(Fig. 9, page 46)*], P2; repeat from ★ across: 34 sts.

**Row 5:** K2, (P1, YO, P1, K2) across: 42 sts.

**Rows 6-43:** Repeat Rows 2-5, 9 times; then repeat Rows 2 and 3 once **more**.

**Row 44:** P2 tog *(Fig. 10, page 46)*, ★ slip 1 as if to **knit**, K2, PSSO, P2 tog; repeat from ★ across: 25 sts.

**Row 45:** K1, (P1, YO, P1, K1) across: 33 sts.

**Row 46:** P1, (K3, P1) across.

**Row 47:** K1, (P3, K1) across.

**Row 48:** P1, ★ [slip 1 as if to **knit**, K2 tog, PSSO *(Fig. 8, page 46)*], P1; repeat from ★ across: 17 sts.

**Row 49:** K1, P2 tog across: 9 sts.

Cut yarn, leaving a long end for sewing. Thread yarn needle with long end and weave through remaining sts to form a ring; pull tightly and secure end, then sew seam from top of Body to last 4 "cables." Sew Ribbing from cast on edge to top of Ribbing, leaving an opening for thumb.

## THUMB
With smaller size knitting needles, cast on one st.

**Row 1** (Right side): Purl increase *(Fig. 4, page 45)*: 2 sts.

**Row 2:** K1, knit increase *(Figs. 3a & b, page 45)*: 3 sts.

**Row 3:** K1, P1, purl increase: 4 sts.

**Row 4:** P1, K2, purl increase: 5 sts.

**Row 5:** K2, P2, knit increase: 6 sts.

**Row 6:** P2, K2, P1, purl increase: 7 sts.

*Instructions continued on page 34.*

**Row 7:** P1, K2, P2, K1, knit increase: 8 sts.

**Row 8:** K1, P2, K2, P2, knit increase: 9 sts.

**Row 9:** (P2, K2) twice, purl increase: 10 sts.

**Row 10:** (K2, P2) twice, K1, knit increase: 11 sts.

**Row 11:** K1, (P2, K2) twice, P1, purl increase: 12 sts.

**Row 12:** P1, K2, (P2, K2) twice, purl increase: 13 sts.

**Row 13:** (K2, P2) 3 times, knit increase: 14 sts.

**Row 14:** (P2, K2) 3 times, P1, purl increase: 15 sts.

**Row 15:** P1, (K2, P2) 3 times, K1, knit increase: 16 sts.

Place a marker around the first and the last st on Row 15 to mark the base of the thumb seam.

**Row 16:** K1, P2, (K2, P2) 3 times, K1.

**Row 17:** P1, K2, (P2, K2) 3 times, P1.

**Rows 18-23:** Repeat Rows 16 and 17, 3 times.

**Row 24:** K1, P2, (K2 tog, P2) 3 times, K1: 13 sts.

**Row 25:** P1, (K2, P1) across.

**Row 26:** K1, (P2, K1) across.

**Rows 27-30:** Repeat Rows 25 and 26 twice.

**Row 31:** P1, K2 tog across: 7 sts.

Cut yarn, leaving a long end for sewing. Thread yarn needle with long end and weave through remaining sts to form a ring; pull tightly and secure end, then sew seam from top of Thumb to marker at base of Thumb. Sew Thumb into opening easing it to fit.

*Designs by Carol Brill.*

## NECK RIBBING

With **right** side facing, using smaller size knitting needles and White, and beginning **after** bound off sts, pick up 14{16-18} sts evenly spaced across Right Front neck edge *(Figs. 13a & b, page 47)*, knit 23{25-27} sts from Back neck st holder, pick up 14{16-18} sts evenly spaced across Left Front neck edge (do **not** pick up sts in bound off edge): 51{57-63} sts.

**Row 1:** K1, (P1, K1) across.

**Row 2:** P1, (K1, P1) across.

**Rows 3-6:** Repeat Rows 1 and 2 twice.

**Row 7:** Work across increasing 10 sts evenly spaced: 61{67-73} sts.

## HOOD

Change to larger size knitting needles.

**Rows 1-4:** Work in Stockinette Stitch for 4 rows.

**Row 5:** Slip 4{3-2}, with next new color K5, (slip 3, K5) across to last 4{3-2} sts, leave last 4{3-2} sts unworked; **turn.**

**Row 6:** K5, (slip 3, K5) across to last 4{3-2} sts, slip 4{3-2}; cut new color.

**Rows 7-10:** With White, work in Stockinette Stitch for 4 rows.

**Row 11:** K 29{32-35}, increase in next st *(Figs. 3a & b, page 45)*, K1, increase in next st, knit across: 63{69-75} sts.

**Row 12:** Purl across.

**Row 13:** Slip 1, with next new color K4{3-2}, slip 3, (K5, slip 3) 2{3-3} times, K6{7-6}, slip 3, K6{5-6}, slip 3, (K5, slip 3) 2{2-3} times, K4{3-2}, leave last st unworked; **turn.**

**Row 14:** K4{3-2}, slip 3, (K5, slip 3) 2{3-3} times, K6{7-6}, slip 3, K6{5-6}, slip 3, (K5, slip 3) 2{2-3} times, K4{3-2}, slip 1; cut new color.

**Rows 15-20:** With White, work in Stockinette Stitch for 6 rows.

**Row 21:** Slip 4{3-2}, with next new color (K5, slip 3) 3{3-4} times, K7{6-7}, slip 3, K5{6-5}, (slip 3, K5) 2{3-3} times, leave remaining 4{3-2} sts unworked; **turn.**

**Row 22:** (K5, slip 3) 3{3-4} times, K7{6-7}, slip 3, K5{6-5}, (slip 3, K5) 2{3-3} times, slip 4{3-2}; cut new color.

**Row 23:** With White K 30{33-36}, increase in next st, K1, increase in next st, knit across: 65{71-77} sts.

**Rows 24-28:** Work in Stockinette Stitch for 5 rows.

**Row 29:** Slip 1, with next new color K4{3-2}, slip 3, (K5, slip 3) 2{2-3} times, K7, slip 3, K7{5-7}, slip 3, K5{7-5}, slip 3, (K5, slip 3) 1{2-2} time(s), K4{3-2}, leave remaining st unworked; **turn.**

**Row 30:** K4{3-2}, slip 3, (K5, slip 3) 2{2-3} times, K7, slip 3, K7{5-7}, slip 3, K5{7-5}, slip 3, (K5, slip 3) 1{2-2} time(s), K4{3-2}, slip 1; cut new color.

**Rows 31 and 32:** With White, work in Stockinette Stitch for 2 rows.

**Row 33:** K 31{34-37}, increase in next st, K1, increase in next st, knit across: 67{73-79} sts.

**Rows 34-36:** Work in Stockinette Stitch for 3 rows.

**Row 37:** Slip 4{3-2}, with next new color (K5, slip 3) 3{3-4} times, K4, slip 3, K4{5-4}, slip 3, K5{4-5}, (slip 3, K5) 2{3-3} times, leave remaining 4{3-2} sts unworked; **turn.**

**Row 38:** (K5, slip 3) 3{3-4} times, K4, slip 3, K4{5-4}, slip 3, K5{4-5}, (slip 3, K5) 2{3-3} times, slip 4{3-2}; cut new color.

**Rows 39-42:** With White, work in Stockinette Stitch for 4 rows.

**Row 43:** K 32{35-38}, increase in next st, K1, increase in next st, knit across: 69{75-81} sts.

**Row 44:** Purl across.

**Row 45:** Slip 1, with next new color, K4{3-2}, slip 3, (K5, slip 3) across to last 5{4-3} sts, K4{3-2}, leave remaining st unworked; **turn.**

**Row 46:** K4{3-2}, slip 3, (K5, slip 3) across to last 5{4-3} sts, K4{3-2}, slip 1; cut new color.

**Rows 47-52:** With White, work in Stockinette Stitch for 6 rows.

**Row 53:** Slip 4{3-2}, with next new color K5, (slip 3, K5) across to last 4{3-2} sts, leave last 4{3-2} sts unworked; **turn.**

**Row 54:** K5, (slip 3, K5) across to last 4{3-2} sts, slip 4{3-2}; cut new color.

Work even until Hood measures approximately 6¹/₂{7-7¹/₂}"/16.5{18-19} cm from top of Neck Ribbing, ending by working a **wrong** side row.

**SHAPING**
Maintain established pattern throughout.

**Row 1:** Work across 33{36-39} sts, [slip 1 as if to **knit**, K2 tog, PSSO *(Fig. 8, page 46)*], work across: 67{73-79} sts.

*Instructions continued on page 36.*

**Row 2:** Work across 32{35-38} sts, P3 tog *(Fig. 12, page 46)*, work across: 65{71-77} sts.

**Row 3:** Work across 31{34-37} sts, slip 1 as if to **knit**, K2 tog, PSSO, work across: 63{69-75} sts.

**Row 4:** Work across 30{33-36} sts, P3 tog, work across: 61{67-73} sts.

Bind off remaining sts.

Fold Hood in half with decreases at fold; sew seam.

## HOOD RIBBING

With **right** side facing, using smaller size knitting needles and White, pick up 91{97-103} sts evenly spaced across Neck Ribbing and Hood.

**Row 1:** P1, (K1, P1) across.

**Row 2 (Right side):** K1, (P1, K1) across.

**Rows 3-15:** Repeat Rows 1 and 2, 6 times; then repeat Row 1 once **more**.

Bind off all sts **loosely** in ribbing.

Fold ribbing in half to inside and sew bound off edge **loosely** in place, forming a casing.

Sew each end of Rows 8-15 to bound off edge of Neck Shaping.

To make a twisted cord, cut four 36" (91.5 cm) lengths of yarn in desired colors. Holding all four strands together, fasten one end to a stationary object **or** have another person hold it; twist until **tight**. Fold in half and let it twist upon itself, knot both ends and cut the loops on the folded end.
Weave the twisted cord through the casing.

## SLEEVE (Make 2)
### RIBBING
With smaller size knitting needles and White, cast on 37{39-41} sts **loosely**.

**Row 1:** P2, K1, (P1, K1) across to last 2 sts, P2.

**Row 2:** K2, P1, (K1, P1) across to last 2 sts, K2.

**Rows 3-10:** Repeat Rows 1 and 2, 4 times.

**Row 11:** Work across increasing 6{4-6} sts evenly spaced: 43{43-47} sts.

## BODY
Change to larger size knitting needles.

**Row 1:** With next new color, K2, slip 3, (K1, slip 3) across to last 2 sts, K2.

**Row 2:** P3, (slip 1, P3) across.

**Row 3:** Knit across.

**Row 4:** Purl across.

**Row 5:** With next new color increase in first st, K1, slip 3, (K1, slip 3) across to last 2 sts, increase in next st, K1: 45{45-49} sts.

**Row 6:** P4, slip 1, (P3, slip 1) across to last 4 sts, P4.

**Row 7:** Knit across.

**Row 8:** Purl across.

**Row 9:** With next new color increase in first st, K2, slip 3, (K1, slip 3) across to last 3 sts, K1, increase in next st, K1: 47{47-51} sts.

**Row 10:** P5, slip 1, (P3, slip 1) across to last 5 sts, P5.

**Row 11:** Knit across.

**Row 12:** Purl across.

**Row 13:** With White increase in first st, knit across to last 2 sts, increase in next st, K1: 49{49-53} sts.

**Rows 14-16:** Work in Stockinette Stitch for 3 rows.

**Row 17:** Increase in first st, knit across to last 2 sts, increase in next st, K1: 51{51-55} sts.

**Row 18:** Purl across.

**Row 19:** Slip 3{3-5}, with next new color K5, (slip 3, K5) across to last 3{3-5} sts, leave last 3{3-5} sts unworked; **turn.**

**Row 20:** K5, (slip 3, K5) across to last 3{3-5} sts, slip 3{3-5}; cut new color.

**Rows 21 and 22:** With White, work in Stockinette Stitch for 2 rows.

**Row 23:** Increase in first st, knit across to last 2 sts, increase in next st, K1: 53{53-57} sts.

**Rows 24-26:** Work in Stockinette Stitch for 3 rows.

**Row 27:** Slip 1{1-2}, with next new color, K4{4-5}, slip 3, (K5, slip 3) across to last 5{5-7} sts, K4{4-5}, leave last 1{1-2} st(s) unworked; **turn.**

**Row 28:** K4{4-5}, slip 3, (K5, slip 3) across to last 5{5-7} sts, K4{4-5}, slip 1{1-2}; cut new color.

Continue in pattern, increasing one st at each edge in same manner, every fourth row, 0{3-0} times **more;** then increase every sixth row, 0{0-3} times: 53{59-63} sts.

Work even until Sleeve measures approximately 6$\frac{1}{2}${7$\frac{1}{2}$-9$\frac{1}{2}$}"/16.5{19-24} cm from cast on edge, ending by working a **wrong** side row.

Bind off all sts **loosely.**

Weave underarm seam *(Fig. 14, page 47).* Set Sleeve into armhole and sew in place.

# FINISHING
Work Buttonhole Band on Right Front for girls or on Left Front for boys.

## BUTTONHOLE BAND
With **right** side facing, using smaller size knitting needles and White, pick up 63{73-85} sts evenly spaced across front edge.

**Row 1 (Wrong side):** P1, (K1, P1) across.

**Row 2:** K1, (P1, K1) across.

**Row 3:** P1, (K1, P1) across.

**Row 4 (Buttonhole row):** K1, P1, K1, YO *(see Yarn Overs, page 44),* K2 tog, ★ work across next 9{11-9} sts, YO, K2 tog; repeat from ★ across to last 3 sts, K1, P1, K1.

**Rows 5-7:** Repeat Rows 1-3.

Bind off all sts in ribbing.

## BUTTON BAND
With **right** side facing, using smaller size knitting needles and White, pick up 63{73-85} sts evenly spaced across front edge.

**Row 1 (Wrong side):** P1, (K1, P1) across.

**Row 2:** K1, (P1, K1) across.

**Rows 3-7:** Repeat Rows 1 and 2 twice, then repeat Row 1 once **more.**

Bind off all sts in ribbing.

Sew buttons to Button Band opposite buttonholes.

*Designed by Joan Beebe.*

## NECK SHAPING

**Row 1:** P5{7-7-7} sts, slip sts just worked onto a st holder, work across: 19{20-22-23} sts.

**Row 2:** Work across to last 2 sts, K2 tog: 18{19-21-22} sts.

**Rows 3 and 4:** Work across.

Bind off remaining sts in pattern.

## LEFT SLEEVE
### RIBBING

With Yellow and straight knitting needles, cast on 30{32-34-36} sts **loosely**.

Work in K1, P1 ribbing for 1½" (4 cm) increasing 16{16-18-18} sts evenly spaced across last row: 46{48-52-54} sts.

### BODY

Change to circular knitting needles.

With Spot Print, work in Stockinette Stitch until Left Sleeve measures approximately 5{6-7-9}"/12.5{15-18-23} cm from cast on edge, ending by working a **purl** row.

Bind off all sts **loosely**.

## RIGHT SLEEVE
### RIBBING

With Peach and straight knitting needles, cast on 30{32-34-36} sts **loosely**.

Work in K1, P1 ribbing for 1½" (4 cm) increasing 16{16-18-18} sts evenly spaced across last row: 46{48-52-54} sts.

### BODY

Change to circular knitting needle.

With Spot Print, work in Stockinette Stitch until Right Sleeve measures approximately 5{6-7-9}"/12.5{15-18-23} cm from cast on edge, ending by working a **purl** row.

Bind off all sts **loosely**.

## FINISHING

Sew shoulder seams.
Weave Sleeve seams *(Fig. 14, page 47)*.
Set Sleeves into armhole and sew in place.

### LEFT BACK YOKE RIBBING

With **right** side facing, using straight knitting needles and Mint, pick up 20{22-24-26} sts evenly spaced across Yoke edge *(Figs. 13a & b, page 47)*.

**Rows 1-7:** (K1, P1) across.

Bind off all sts in ribbing.

### RIGHT BACK YOKE RIBBING

With **right** side facing, using straight knitting needles and Mint, pick up 20{22-24-26} sts evenly spaced across Yoke edge.

**Rows 1-3:** (K1, P1) across.

**Row 4** (Buttonhole row): Work across 6{8-8-8} sts, ★ K2 tog, YO *(see Yarn Overs, page 44)*, work across next 5{5-6-7} sts; repeat from ★ once **more**.

**Rows 5-7:** (K1, P1) across.

Bind off all sts in ribbing.

### NECK RIBBING

With **right** side facing, using straight knitting needles and Blue, pick up 6 sts along edge of Left Back Yoke Ribbing, K5{7-7-7} sts from st holder, pick up 12{13-13-13} sts along left neck edge, slip 12{16-16-16} from Front st holder onto empty knitting needle and knit across, pick up 13{14-14-14} sts along right neck edge, slip 5{7-7-7} sts from st holder onto empty knitting needle and knit across, pick up 6 sts along Right Back Yoke Ribbing: 59{69-69-69} sts.

**Row 1:** P1, (K1, P1) across.

**Row 2:** K1, (P1, K1) across.

**Row 3:** P1, (K1, P1) across.

**Row 4 (Buttonhole row):** K1, (P1, K1) across to last 4 sts, YO, K2 tog, P1, K1.

**Rows 5-7:** Repeat Rows 1-3.

Bind off all sts **loosely** in ribbing.

## FRONT INNER LEG RIBBING

With **right** side facing, using straight knitting needles and Mint, pick up 87{101-113-127} sts evenly spaced across inner leg edge of Front.

**Row 1:** P1, (K1, P1) across.

**Row 2:** K1, (P1, K1) across.

**Rows 3-7:** Repeat Rows 1 and 2 twice, then repeat Row 1 once **more**.

Bind off all sts in ribbing.

## BACK INNER LEG RIBBING

With **right** side facing, using straight knitting needles and Yellow, pick up 87{101-113-127} sts evenly spaced across inner leg edge of Back.

Complete same as Front Inner Leg Ribbing.

Sew female side of snap tape to **wrong** side of Front Inner Leg Ribbing; sew male side of snap tape to **right** side of Back Inner Leg Ribbing. Sew edge of Yoke ribbing to bound off sts at base of Yoke.
Sew buttons to Left Back Yoke Ribbing opposite buttonholes.

*Designed by Joan Beebe.*

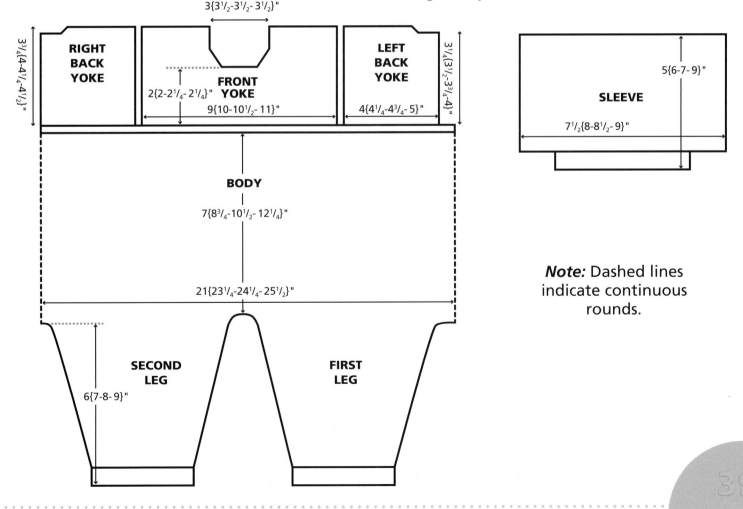

*Note:* Dashed lines indicate continuous rounds.

# thank you for helping
# warm up
## america!

Since 1991, Warm Up America! has donated more than 250,000 afghans to battered women's shelters, victims of natural disaster, the homeless, and many others who are in need.

You can help Warm Up America! help others, and with so little effort. Debbie urges everyone who uses the patterns in this book to take a few minutes to knit a 7" x 9" block for this worthy cause. To help you get started, she's providing this block pattern.

If you are able to provide a completed afghan, Warm Up America requests that you donate it directly to any charity or social services agency in your community. If you require assistance in assembling the blocks into an afghan, please include your name and address inside the packaging and ship your 7" x 9" blocks to:

Warm Up America! Foundation
2500 Lowell Road
Ranlo, NC 28054

Remember, just a little bit of yarn can make a big difference to someone in need!

*Basic patchwork afghans are made of forty-nine 7" x 9" (18 cm x 23 cm) rectangular blocks that are sewn together. Any pattern stitch can be used for the rectangle. Use acrylic medium weight yarn and size 8 (5 mm) straight knitting needles or size needed to obtain the gauge of 9 stitches to 2" (5 cm).*

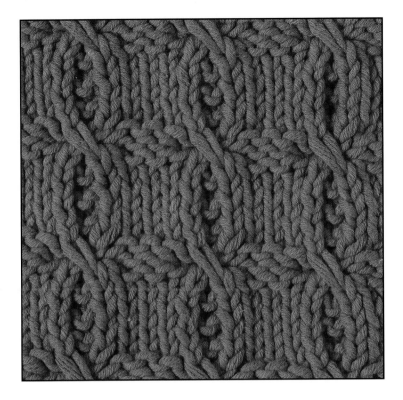

**Row 8:** (K2, WYF slip 1) twice, (K3, WYF slip 1, K2, WYF slip 1) across to last 2 sts, K2.

**Row 9:** K2, slip next st onto cable needle and hold in **front** of work, knit third st on left needle making sure not to drop off, then knit first and second sts letting all 3 sts drop off left needle, K1 from cable needle, ★ K3, slip next st onto cable needle and hold in **front** of work, knit third st on left needle making sure not to drop off, then knit first and second sts letting all 3 sts drop off left needle, K1 from cable needle; repeat from ★ across to last 2 sts, K2.

**Row 10:** P3, K2, (P5, K2) across to last 3 sts, P3.

Repeat Rows 1-10 for pattern until Block measures approximately 9" (23 cm) from cast on edge, ending by working a **wrong** side row.

Bind off all sts in pattern.

# SLIP STITCH BOXES BLOCK

Multiple of 7 sts + 1.

**Additional materials:** Cable needle

When instructed to slip a stitch, always slip as if to **purl**.

Cast on 36 sts.

**Row 1** (Right side)**:** Knit across.

**Row 2:** P3, K2, (P5, K2) across to last 3 sts, P3.

**Row 3:** Knit across.

**Rows 4 and 5:** Repeat Rows 2 and 3.

**Row 6:** (K2, WYF slip 1) twice, (K3, WYF slip 1, K2, WYF slip 1) across to last 2 sts, K2.

**Row 7:** P2, WYB slip 1, K2, WYB slip 1, (P3, WYB slip 1, K2, WYB slip 1) across to last 2 sts, P2.

## ABBREVIATIONS

| | |
|---|---|
| C2B | Cable 2 Back |
| C2F | Cable 2 Front |
| cm | centimeters |
| K | knit |
| mm | millimeters |
| P | purl |
| PSSO | pass slipped stitch over |
| P2SSO | pass 2 slipped stitches over |
| Rnd(s) | Round(s) |
| st(s) | stitch(es) |
| tbl | through back loop |
| tog | together |
| WYF | with yarn forward |
| WYB | with yarn back |
| YO | yarn over |

★ — work instructions following ★ as many **more** times as indicated in addition to the first time.

† to † — work all instructions from first † to second † **as many** times as specified.

( ) or [ ] — work enclosed instructions as many times as specified by the number immediately following **or** work all enclosed instructions in stitch or space indicated or contains explanatory remarks.

colon (:) — the number(s) given after a colon at the end of a row or round denote(s) the number of stitches or spaces you should have on that row or round.

## GAUGE

Exact gauge is **essential** for proper size. Needle size(s) given in instructions is/are merely a guide and should never be used without first making a sample swatch approximately 4" (10 cm) square in the stitch, yarn, and needles specified. Then measure it, counting your stitches and rows carefully. If your swatch is larger or smaller than specified, **make another, changing needle size to get the correct gauge**. Keep trying until you find the size needles that will give you the specified gauge.

## MARKERS

As a convenience to you, we have used markers to help distinguish the beginning of a round or pattern. Place markers as instructed. You may use purchased markers or tie a length of contrasting color yarn around the needle. When you reach the marker on each row or round, slip it from the left needle to the right needle; remove it when no longer needed.

## ZEROS

To consolidate the length of an involved pattern, Zeros are sometimes used so that all sizes can be combined. For example, slip 2{3-0} means that the first size would slip 2, the second size would slip 3, and the largest size would do nothing.

| KNIT & CROCHET TERMINOLOGY | |
|---|---|
| **UNITED STATES** | **INTERNATIONAL** |
| gauge = | tension |
| bind off = | cast off |
| yarn over (YO) = | yarn forward (yfwd) **or** yarn around needle (yrn) |
| slip stitch (slip st) = | single crochet (sc) |
| single crochet (sc) = | double crochet (dc) |

| Yarn Weight Symbol & Names | SUPER FINE 1 | FINE 2 | LIGHT 3 | MEDIUM 4 | BULKY 5 | SUPER BULKY 6 |
|---|---|---|---|---|---|---|
| Type of Yarns in Category | Sock, Fingering Baby | Sport, Baby | DK, Light Worsted | Worsted, Afghan, Aran | Chunky, Craft, Rug | Bulky, Roving |
| Knit Gauge Ranges in Stockinette St to 4" (10 cm) | 27-32 sts | 23-26 sts | 21-24 sts | 16-20 sts | 12-15 sts | 6-11 sts |
| Advised Needle Size Range | 1-3 | 3-5 | 5-7 | 7-9 | 9-11 | 11 and larger |

| KNITTING NEEDLES | | | | | | | | | | | | | | | | |
|---|---|---|---|---|---|---|---|---|---|---|---|---|---|---|---|---|
| U.S. | 0 | 1 | 2 | 3 | 4 | 5 | 6 | 7 | 8 | 9 | 10 | 10½ | 11 | 13 | 15 | 17 |
| U.K. | 13 | 12 | 11 | 10 | 9 | 8 | 7 | 6 | 5 | 4 | 3 | 2 | 1 | 00 | 000 | --- |
| Metric - mm | 2 | 2.25 | 2.75 | 3.25 | 3.5 | 3.75 | 4 | 4.5 | 5 | 5.5 | 6 | 6.5 | 8 | 9 | 10 | 12.75 |

| SKILL LEVELS | |
|---|---|
| ●□□□ BEGINNER | Projects for first-time knitters using basic knit and purl stitches. Minimal shaping. |
| ●■□□ EASY | Projects using basic stitches, repetitive stitch patterns, simple color changes, and simple shaping and finishing. |
| ●■■□ INTERMEDIATE | Projects with a variety of stitches, such as basic cables and lace, simple intarsia, double-pointed needles and knitting in the round needle techniques, mid-level shaping and finishing. |
| ●■■■ EXPERIENCED | Projects using advanced techniques and stitches, such as short rows, fair isle, more intricate intarsia, cables, lace patterns, and numerous color changes. |

# YARN OVERS

A yarn over *(abbreviated YO)* is simply placing the yarn over the right needle creating an extra stitch. Since the yarn over produces a hole in the knit fabric, it is used for a lacy effect. On the row following a yarn over, you must be careful to keep it on the needle and treat it as a stitch by knitting or purling it as instructed.

To make a yarn over, you'll loop the yarn over the needle like you would to knit or purl a stitch, bringing it either to the front or the back of the piece so that it'll be ready to work the next stitch, creating a new stitch on the needle as follows:

**After and knit stitch, before a knit stitch**
Bring the yarn forward **between** the needles, then back **over** the top of the right hand needle, so that it is now in position to knit the next stitch *(Fig. 1a)*.

Fig. 1a

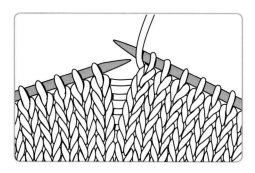

**After a purl stitch, before a purl stitch**
Take the yarn **over** the right hand needle to the back, then forward **between** the needles again, so that it is now in position to purl the next stitch *(Fig. 1b)*.

Fig. 1b

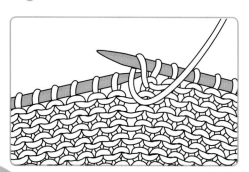

**After a knit stitch, before a purl stitch**
Bring the yarn forward **between** the needles, then back **over** the top of the right hand needle and forward **between** the needles again, so that it is now in position to purl the next stitch *(Fig. 1c)*.

Fig. 1c

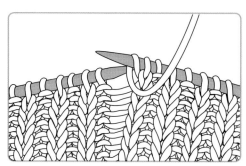

# ADDING NEW STITCHES

Insert the right needle into the stitch as if to **knit**, yarn over and pull the loop through *(Fig. 2a)*, insert the left needle into the loop just worked from **front** to **back** and slip it onto the left needle *(Fig. 2b)*. Repeat for the required number of stitches.

Fig. 2a

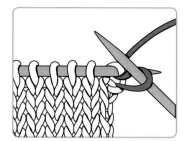

Fig. 2b

# INCREASES

The increases in this book use one stitch to make two stitches. You will have two stitches on the right needle for the one stitch worked off the left needle. The type of increase used depends on the stitch needed to maintain the pattern.

## KNIT INCREASE

Knit the next stitch but do **not** slip the old stitch off the left needle *(Fig. 3a)*. Insert the right needle into the **back** loop of the **same** stitch and knit it *(Fig. 3b)*, then slip the old stitch off the needle.

Fig. 3a

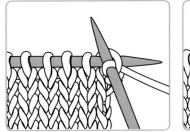

Fig. 3b

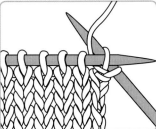

## PURL INCREASE

Purl the next stitch but do **not** slip the old stitch off the left needle. Insert the right needle into the **back** loop of the **same** stitch *(Fig. 4)* and purl it, then slip the old stitch off the left needle.

Fig. 4

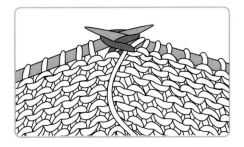

## INCREASING EVENLY

Add one to the number of increases required and divide that number into the number of stitches on the needle. Subtract one from the result and the new number is the approximate number of stitches to be worked between each increase. Adjust the number as needed.

# DECREASES

## KNIT 2 TOGETHER *(abbreviated K2 tog)*

Insert the right needle into the **front** of the first two stitches on the left needle as if to **knit** *(Fig. 5)*, then knit them together as if they were one stitch.

Fig. 5

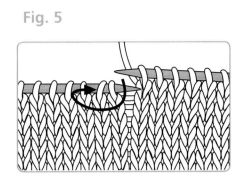

## SLIP, SLIP, KNIT *(abbreviated SSK)*

With yarn in back of the work, separately slip two stitches as if to **knit** *(Fig. 6a)*. Insert the left needle into the **front** of both slipped stitches *(Fig. 6b)* and knit them together as if they were one stitch *(Fig. 6c)*.

Fig. 6a          Fig. 6b

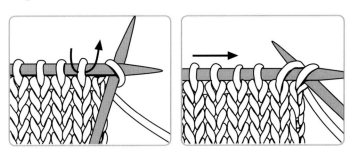

Fig. 6c

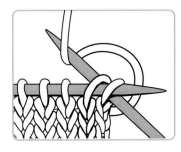

## SLIP 1, KNIT 1, PASS SLIPPED STITCH OVER (abbreviated slip 1, K1, PSSO)

Slip one stitch as if to **knit** (*Fig. 7a*). Knit the next stitch. With the left needle, bring the slipped stitch over the knit stitch (*Fig. 7b*) and off the needle.

Fig. 7a          Fig. 7b

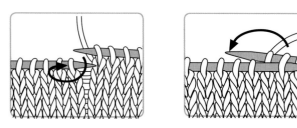

## SLIP 1, KNIT 2 TOGETHER, PASS SLIPPED STITCH OVER
### (abbreviated slip 1, K2 tog, PSSO)

Slip one stitch as if to **knit** (*Fig. 7a*), then knit the next two stitches together (*Fig. 5, page 45*). With the left needle, bring the slipped stitch over the stitch just made (*Fig. 8*) and off the needle.

Fig. 8

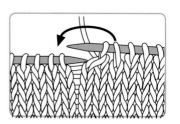

## SLIP 1, KNIT 2, PASS SLIPPED STITCH OVER (abbreviated slip 1, K2, PSSO)

Slip one stitch as if to **knit** (*Fig. 7a*). Knit the next two stitches. With the left needle, bring the slipped stitch over the two knit stitches (*Fig. 9*) and off the needle.

Fig. 9

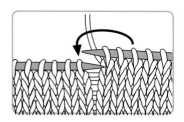

## PURL 2 TOGETHER (abbreviated P2 tog)

Insert the right needle into the **front** of the first two stitches on the left needle as if to **purl** (*Fig. 10*), then purl them together as if they were one stitch.

Fig. 10

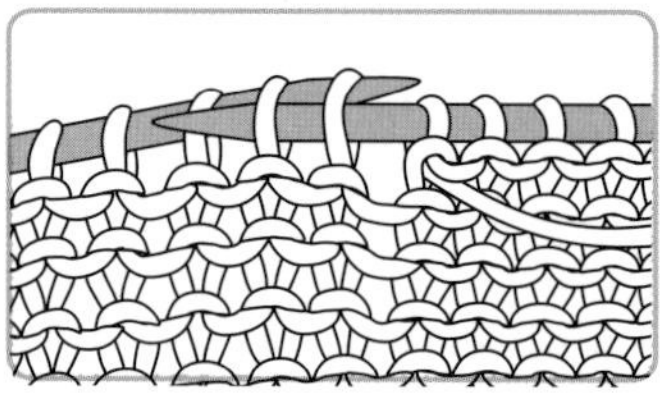

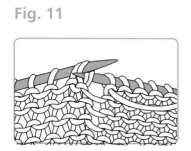

## PURL 2 TOGETHER THROUGH THE BACK LOOP (abbreviated P2 tog tbl)

Insert the right needle into the **back** of both stitches from **back** to **front** (*Fig. 11*), then purl them together as if they were one stitch.

Fig. 11

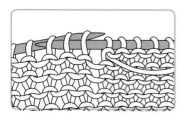

## PURL 3 TOGETHER (abbreviated P3 tog)

Insert the right needle into the **front** of the first three stitches on the left needle as if to **purl** (*Fig. 12*), then purl them together as if they were one stitch.

Fig. 12

# PICKING UP STITCHES

When instructed to pick up stitches, insert the needle from the **front** to the **back** under two strands at the edge of the worked piece **(Figs. 13a & b)**. Put the yarn around the needle as if to **knit**, then bring the needle with the yarn back through the stitch to the right side, resulting in a stitch on the needle.

Repeat this along the edge, picking up the required number of stitches.

A crochet hook may be helpful to pull yarn through.

Fig. 13a

Fig. 13b

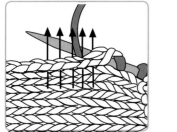
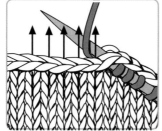

# WEAVING SEAMS

With the **right** side of both pieces facing you and edges even, sew through both pieces once to secure the beginning of the seam, leaving an ample yarn end to weave in later. Insert the needle under the bar **between** the first and second stitches on the row and pull the yarn through **(Fig. 14)**. Insert the needle under the next bar on the second side. Repeat from side to side, being careful to match rows. If the edges are different lengths, it may be necessary to insert the needle under two bars at one edge.

Fig. 14

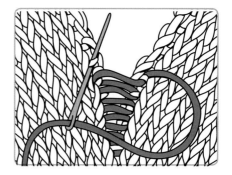

# FRINGE

Cut a piece of cardboard 4" (10 cm) wide and half as long as specified in individual instructions for strands. Wind the yarn **loosely** and **evenly** around the cardboard until the card is filled, then cut across one end; repeat as needed.

Hold together as many strands as specified in individual instruction; fold in half. With **wrong** side facing and using a crochet hook, draw the folded end up through a stitch and pull the loose ends through the folded end **(Fig. 15a)**; draw the knot up **tightly (Fig. 15b)**. Repeat, spacing as specified in individual instructions.

Lay piece on a hard surface and trim the ends.

Fig. 15a

Fig. 15b

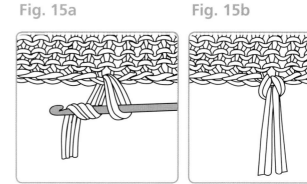

# yarninformation

The projects in this leaflet were made using a variety of yarns. Any brand of yarn in the specified weight may be used. It is best to refer to the yardage/meters when determining how many balls, skeins or hanks to purchase. Remember, to arrive at the finished size and to achieve the same look, it is the GAUGE/TENSION that is important, not the brand of yarn.

For your convenience, listed below are the specific yarns used to create our photography models.

**BEGINNER'S PRAYER SHAWL**
Patons® Shetland Chunky
#03526 Leaf Green

**BABY'S HOODED CARDIGAN**
Berroco's Wendy Peter Pan DK
White - #300 Pure White
Baby Blue - #306 Baby Blue
Pale Yellow - #303 Pale Lemon
Peach - #302 Peach Cream
Lt Green - #304 Watersprite
Lavender - #307 Slumberland
Baby Pink - #305 Baby Pink

**WELCOME, LITTLE ONESIE**
Berroco's Wendy Peter Pan Spot Print DK
Spot Print - #772 Iced Gateau
Berroco's Wendy Peter Pan DK
Peach - #302 Peach Cream
Mint - #304 Watersprite
Yellow - #303 Pale Lemon
Blue - #306 Baby Blue

**KNITTED BEANIE**
Moda Dea™ Washable Wool™
#4453 Tangerine

**YOU'RE INVITED**
DMC® Cébélia
Ecru

**SEATTLE CHILL CHASERS**
Bernat® Berella "4"®
#08940 Natural

**LAP ROBE**
Bernat® Soft Bouclé
#26959 Teal Twist

**LONG ON WARMTH PRAYER SHAWL**
Lion Brand® Wool Ease® Chunky
#135 Spice

**THREE-CORNER PRAYER SHAWL**
Caron® Simply Soft® Shadows
#0007 Mardi Grey

**ALIX'S LACE PRAYER SHAWL**
Blue Moon Fiber Arts Socks that Rock Yarn
Grandmother's Flower Garden Colorway